With love for my twin grandsons,
Michael and John: one is older,
the other is taller, but they hold
equal places in my heart.

–C.C.M.

"He who eats my flesh and drinks my blood has eternal life, and I will raise him up at the last day. For my flesh is food indeed, and my blood is drink indeed."

—John 6:54-55

In accordance with CIC 827, permission to publish has been granted on September 9, 2021, by the Most Reverend Mark S. Rivituso, Auxiliary Bishop, Archdiocese of St. Louis. Permission to publish is an indication that nothing contrary to Church teaching is contained in this particular work. It does not imply any endorsement of the opinions expressed in the publication, or a general endorsement of any author; nor is any liability assumed by this permission.

Published by Ascension Publishing Group, LLC.

Ascension
PO Box 1990
West Chester, PA 19380

1-800-376-0520
ascensionpress.com

Cover design: Rosemary Strohm

Printed in the United States of America
21 22 23 24 25 5 4 3 2 1

ISBN 978-1-950784-63-9

The Real Presence ~~Presents~~

Written by CLAUDIA CANGILLA McADAM

Illustrated by GINA CAPALDI

ASCENSION Kids

West Chester, Pennsylvania

"Grain!" Zedekiah yelled.

"Grapes!" his cousin
Abigail shouted.

2

The two argued about
which was better:
the crop Zedekiah
and his parents grew,
or the fruit farmed by
Abigail's family.

Grain or grapes.
Wheat or wine.

In fact, the cousins tried to outdo each other in everything.

"I'm older."

"Faster."

"I'm taller."

"Stronger."

But this debate about their families' crops had lasted for months. Daily, the disagreement echoed off the stone walls of Capernaum and whipped up whitecaps on the Sea of Galilee.

"We should ask Jesus which is better, grain or grapes," Zedekiah said. "Oh, Zedi," Abigail answered. "He would say grapes. His first miracle turned water into wine."

"Yes, but he fed 5,000 people with just five loaves of bread." Zedekiah puffed out his chest like a peacock.

"When you grow wheat, that's all you get. Bread." Abigail's cheeks dimpled with a crescent on each side. "But we produce grapes, raisins, and wine. Three things, all from one crop!"

"But everyone needs bread!" Zedi said.

Abigail shouldered past her cousin and scurried into the synagogue. It was the Sabbath, and Jesus was going to teach today.

Zedekiah trailed after her. He stood next to Abigail as
silent and straight as a cypress tree. Both eyed Jesus
at the far end of the synagogue. Abigail's fingers snaked
around Zedekiah's wrist, but he snapped his arm free.

The words of Jesus crashed over the crowd like waves.
"I am the living bread which came down from heaven,"
he exclaimed. Bread! Zedi felt his heart thump faster.
He glanced at Abigail.

Jesus continued.
"If anyone eats this bread,
he will live forever!"

Abigail's eyebrows
jumped. Why was
Jesus talking so
much about bread?

People in front of the cousins grumbled. Jesus added, "He who eats my flesh and drinks my blood has eternal life, and I will raise him up at the last day!"

Many of the people in the synagogue tried to shout him down.

Others plugged
their ears.
Large groups slipped
out of the doors.

14

The cousins heard Jesus ask his closest friends if they wanted to leave, too.

One of his disciples, a man named Peter, answered for all of them. "Lord, to whom shall we go? You have the words of eternal life." The cousins decided it wasn't the right time to ask Jesus their question about which of their crops was better.

"What do you think about what Jesus said?" Abigail asked Zedekiah later.

"How could we eat his body? Or drink his blood?" Zedi said. "He must have been joking."

16

Abigail wrinkled her brow. "No one laughed."

"Then he must have been speaking in symbols. Maybe it was an image," said Zedi. "Perhaps he meant that we should accept all of him, all of what he teaches. People just misunderstood."

Abigail shook her head back and forth like the flag flapping on top of the soldiers' fortress. "No, if he meant something different, he would have explained."

"He would have kept them from leaving."

Zedekiah's frown plowed creases across his forehead. "I don't believe what he said. I could never eat *anyone's* flesh or drink their blood."

"I trust him," Abigail said.
"Even if I don't understand how it is possible."

It was almost Passover, and their families were preparing to travel to Jerusalem to celebrate the feast at their aunt's home. Each cousin made something special to bring to the meal. Now the two had another thing to debate. Whose handiwork was finer?

Zedekiah had woven a tray from tall grass gathered at the shore of the Sea of Galilee. "A platter for my bread!"

Abigail had braided silky cord, dyed it poppy red, and twisted it around the handle of her best pouring pitcher.

"For wine! It's pretty," Abigail proclaimed.

Zedekiah replied, "Mine's sturdy."

"Clever!" Abigail argued.

Zedekiah shot back, "Useful!"

On the long journey to Jerusalem, they sat
in the back of the wagon. Zedekiah pressed
his lips together as thin as fishing line.
Abigail's eyes blazed with the fire of twin oil lamps.
Neither spoke a word to the other.

In Jerusalem, their aunt led the families to her upper room
to prepare for the Passover meal. "We have special guests
coming tonight," she said. "Jesus and his apostles!"
Abigail and Zedekiah gasped. They could give
their gifts to the Lord! Zedi's bread on his platter.
Abigail's wine in her pitcher.The contest over
which was better would end tonight.
Jesus would be the judge.

Zedekiah baked unleavened bread from grain he had milled. Abigail tipped a large storage jar and filled her pitcher with wine from grapes she had stomped with the power of a marching army.

That evening, they stood stood next to Jesus' mother, Mary, holding their gifts. "We have presents for the Lord," Zedi told Mary. "We hope he tells us which is better."

Abigail added in a low voice, "And we want to know about what he said in the synagogue in Capernaum. We don't understand."

With a hand on each cousin's back, Mary turned them toward the table. "Do whatever he tells you," she whispered, giving them a little pat to start them walking.

Jesus smiled at the cousins as he took Zedi's platter and Abigail's pitcher. He lifted a circle of bread, so close in color to his skin tone that Zedekiah couldn't tell the difference between Jesus' fingers and the food. "Take, eat. This is my body, which is given for you," Jesus said. "Do this in remembrance of me."

Abigail watched him pick up the pitcher and pour the red wine into his chalice. "Drink of it, all of you," he said as he lifted it. "This is my blood of the new covenant, poured out for many for the forgiveness of sins."

30

As soft as candle smoke, Zedekiah's fingers curled around Abigail's hand. She squeezed back as they locked eyes. Argument had turned to agreement. It didn't matter if bread or wine was better.

The work of their hands had become his Body and Blood. Jesus was giving them himself. They understood now. Jesus had really meant what he said. They only had to believe. And eat and drink.